My Best Pet

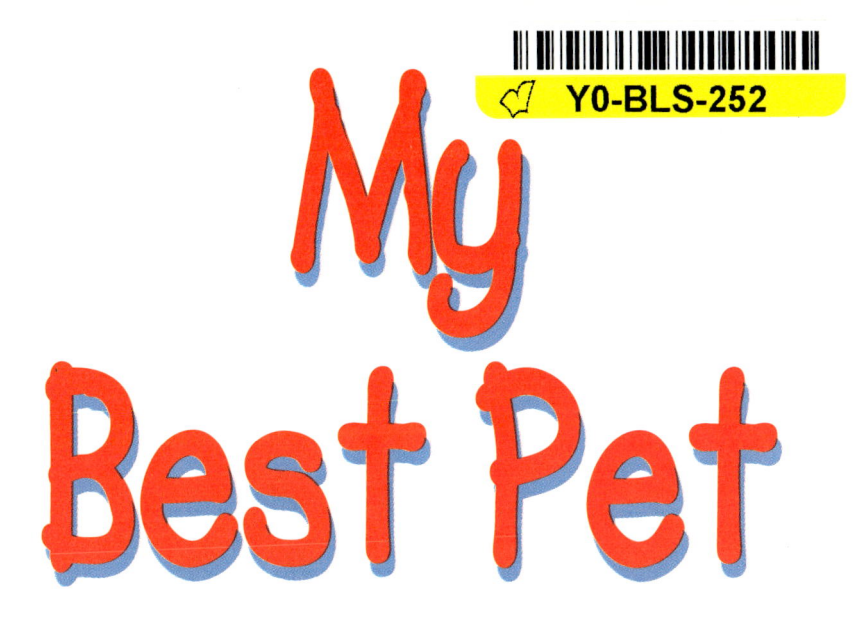

Gordon Winch & Gregory Blaxell
Illustrated by Jean Mulligan

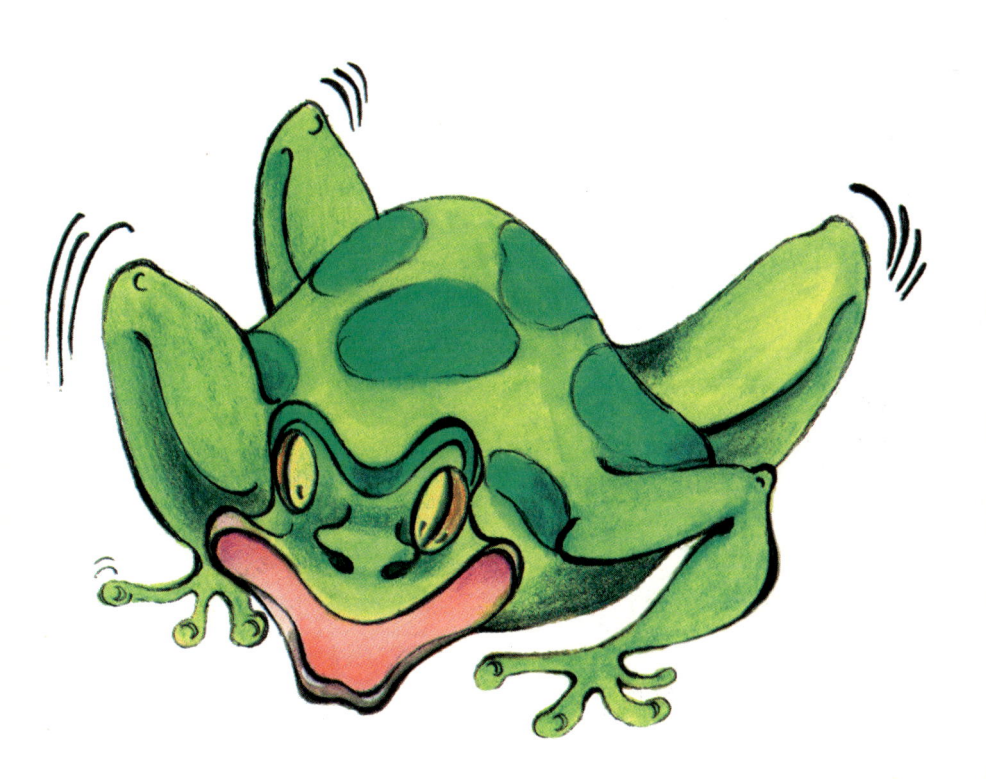

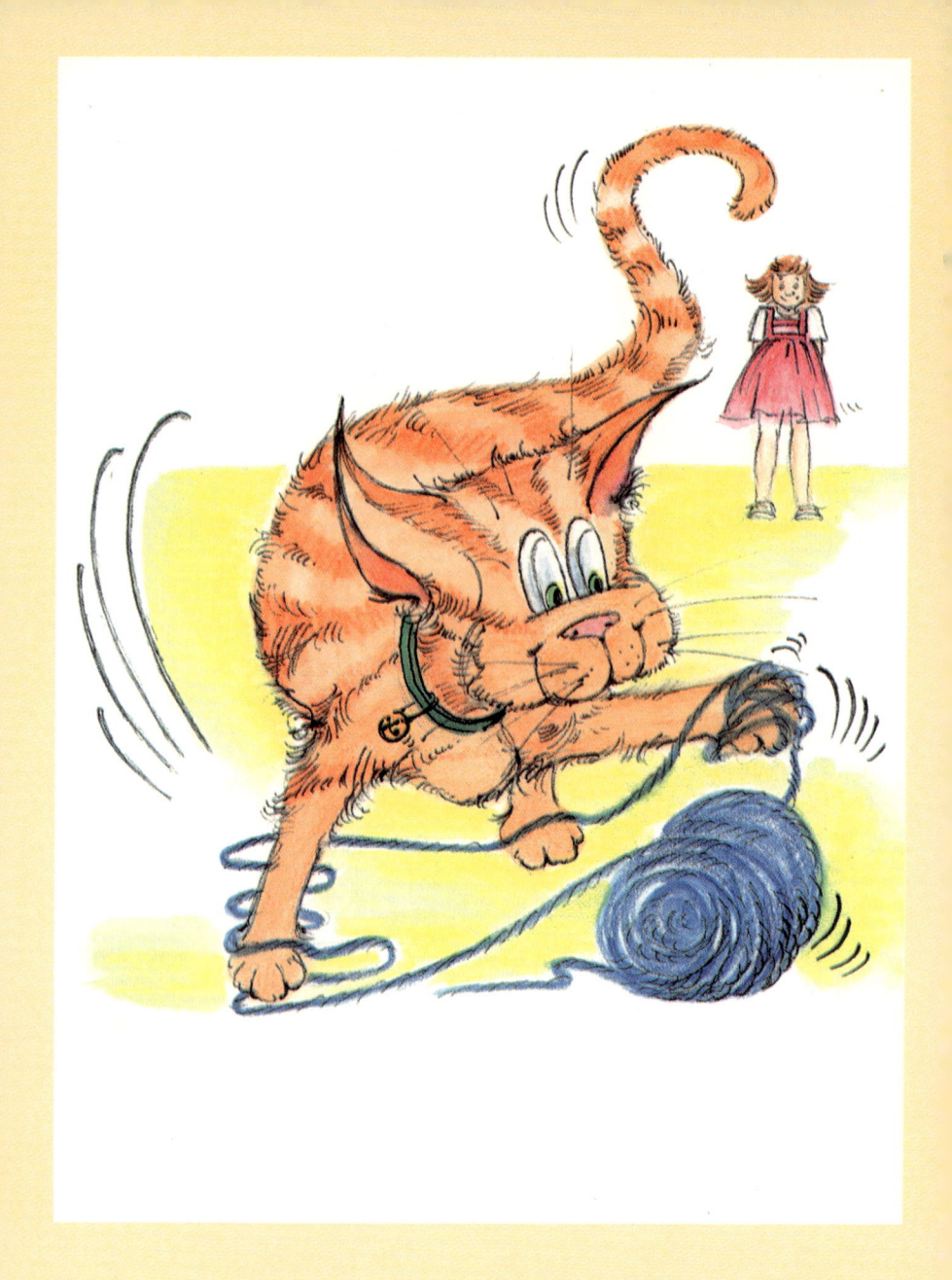

I've got a pet cat.

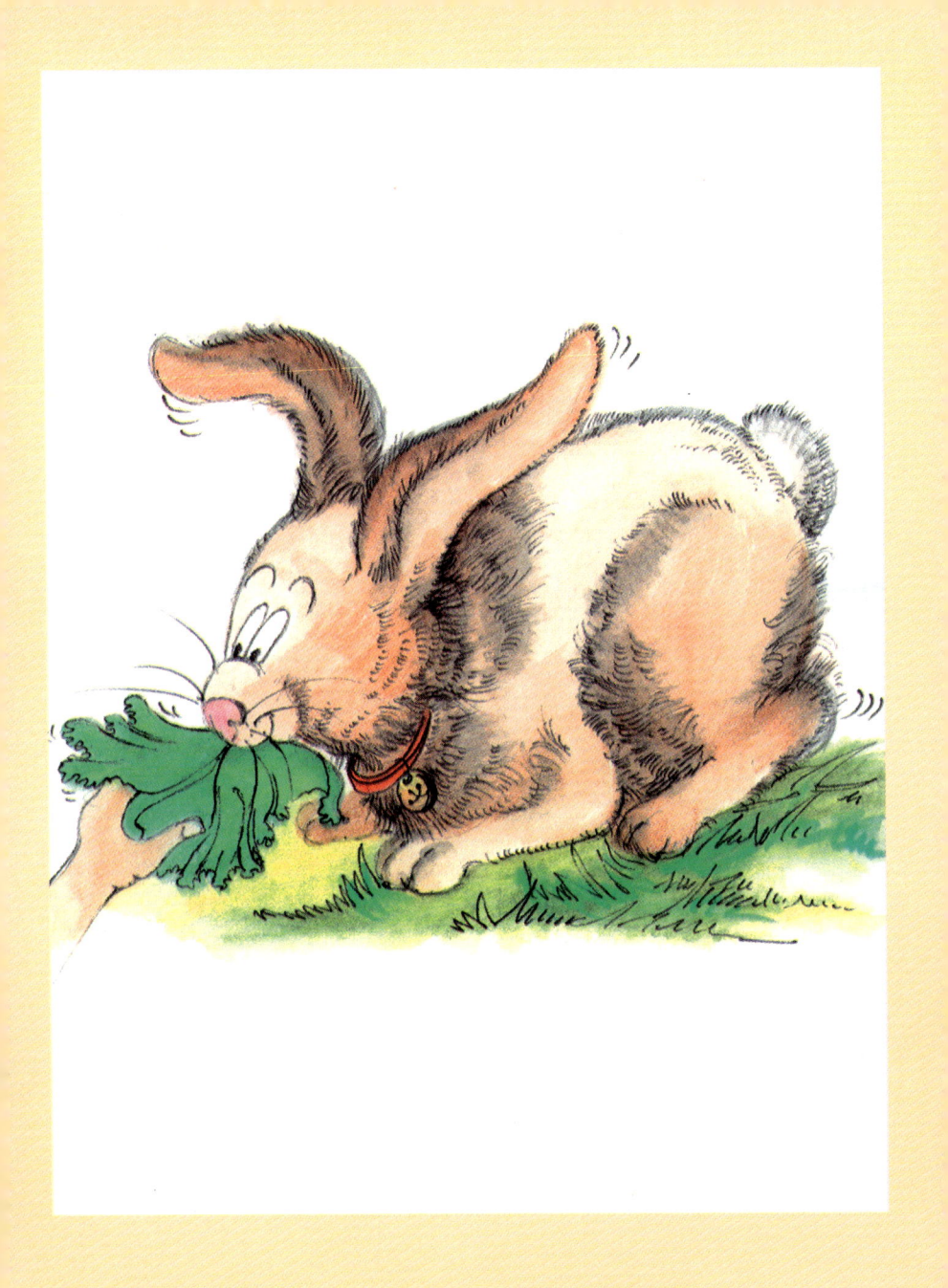

I've got a pet rabbit.

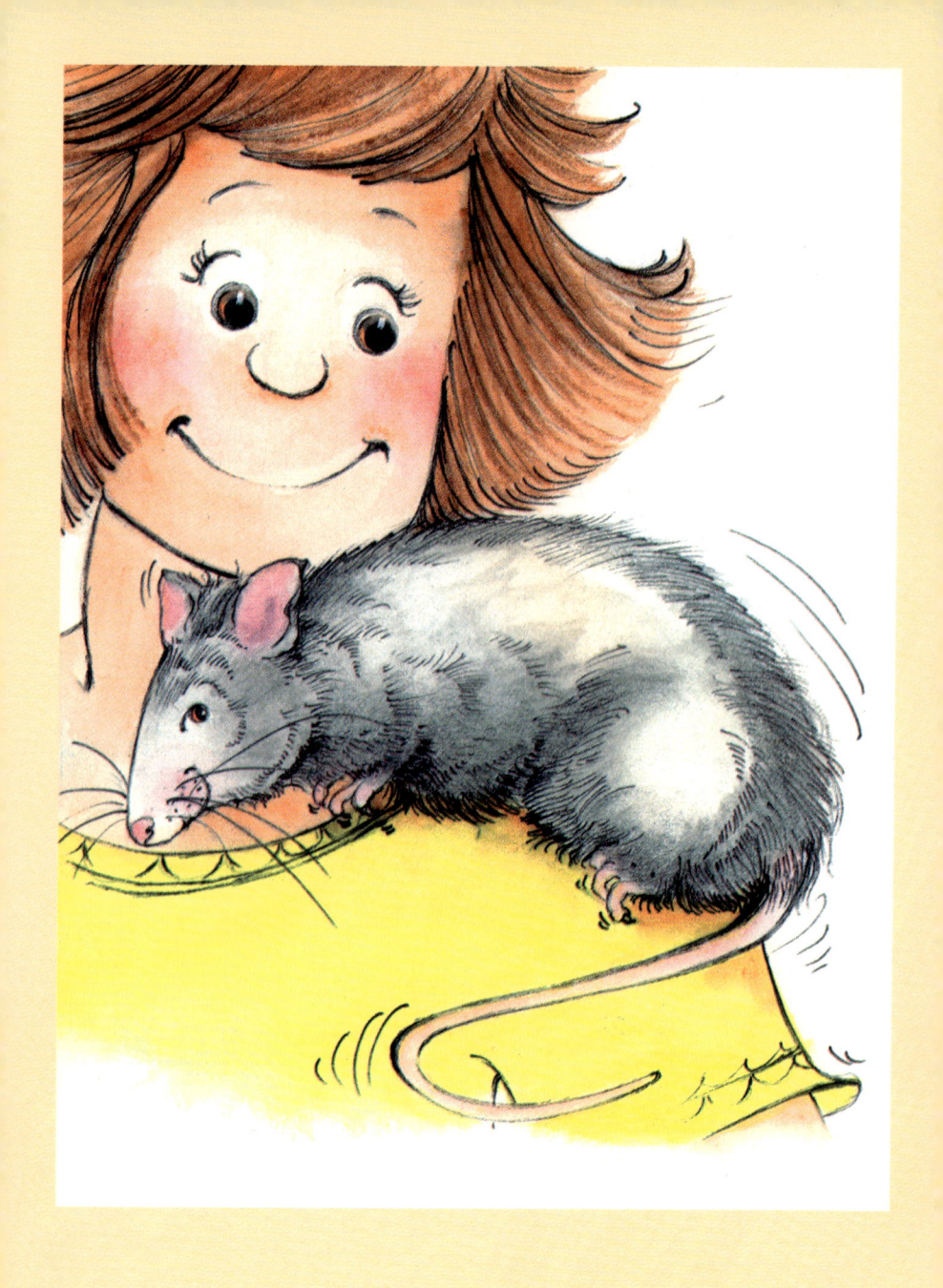

I've got a pet rat

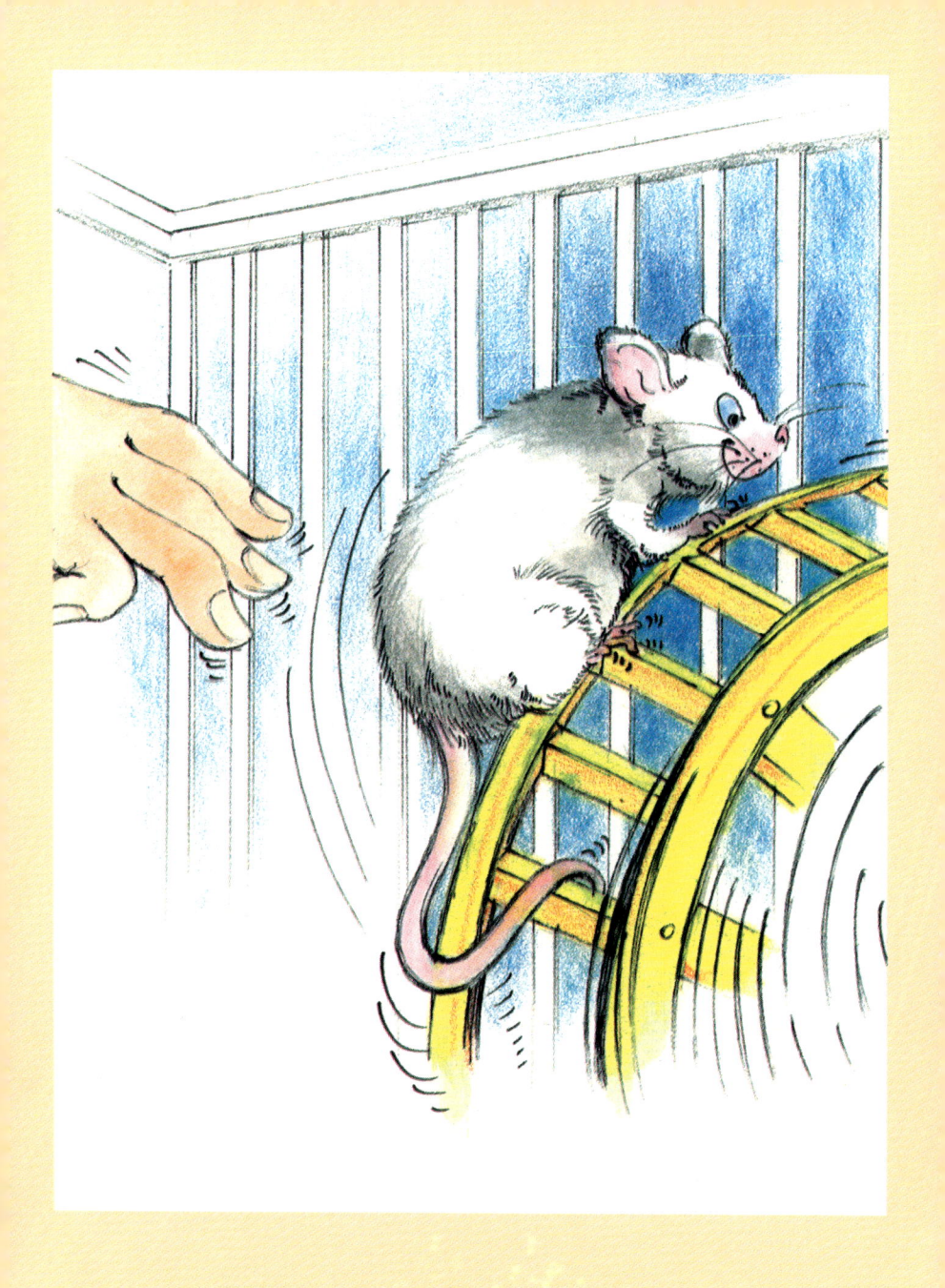

and a pet mouse.

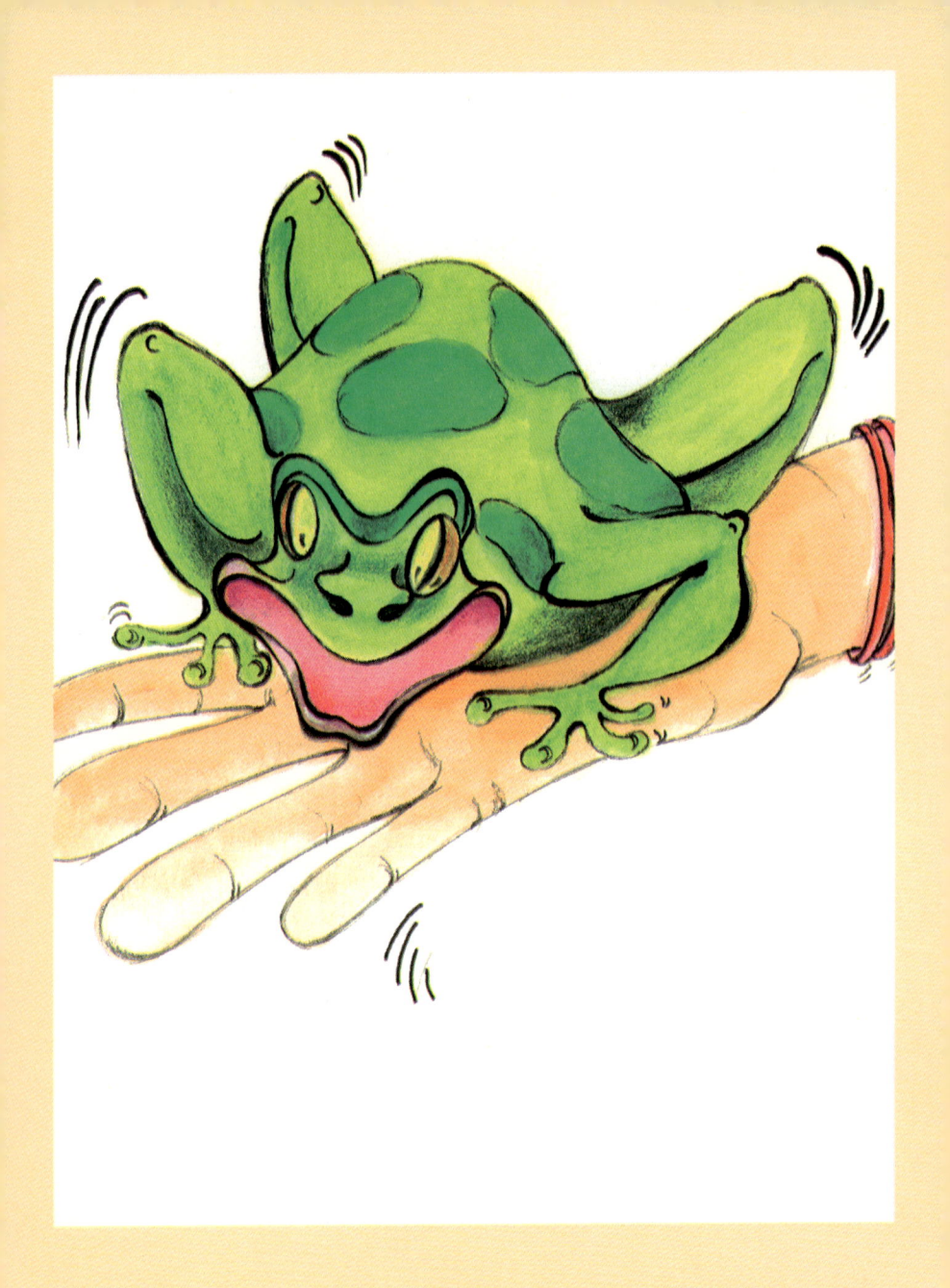

I've got a pet frog

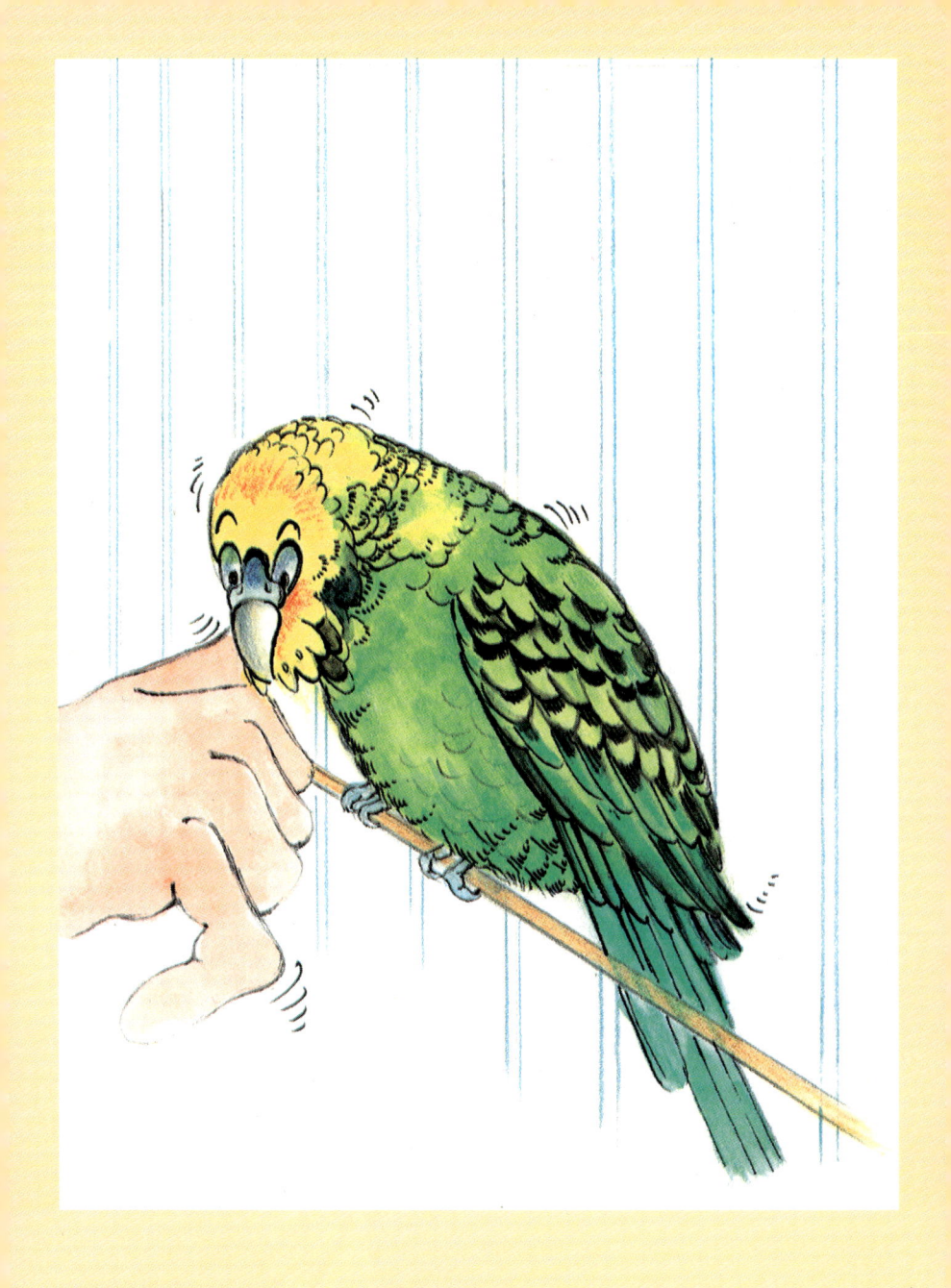

and a pet bird but . . .

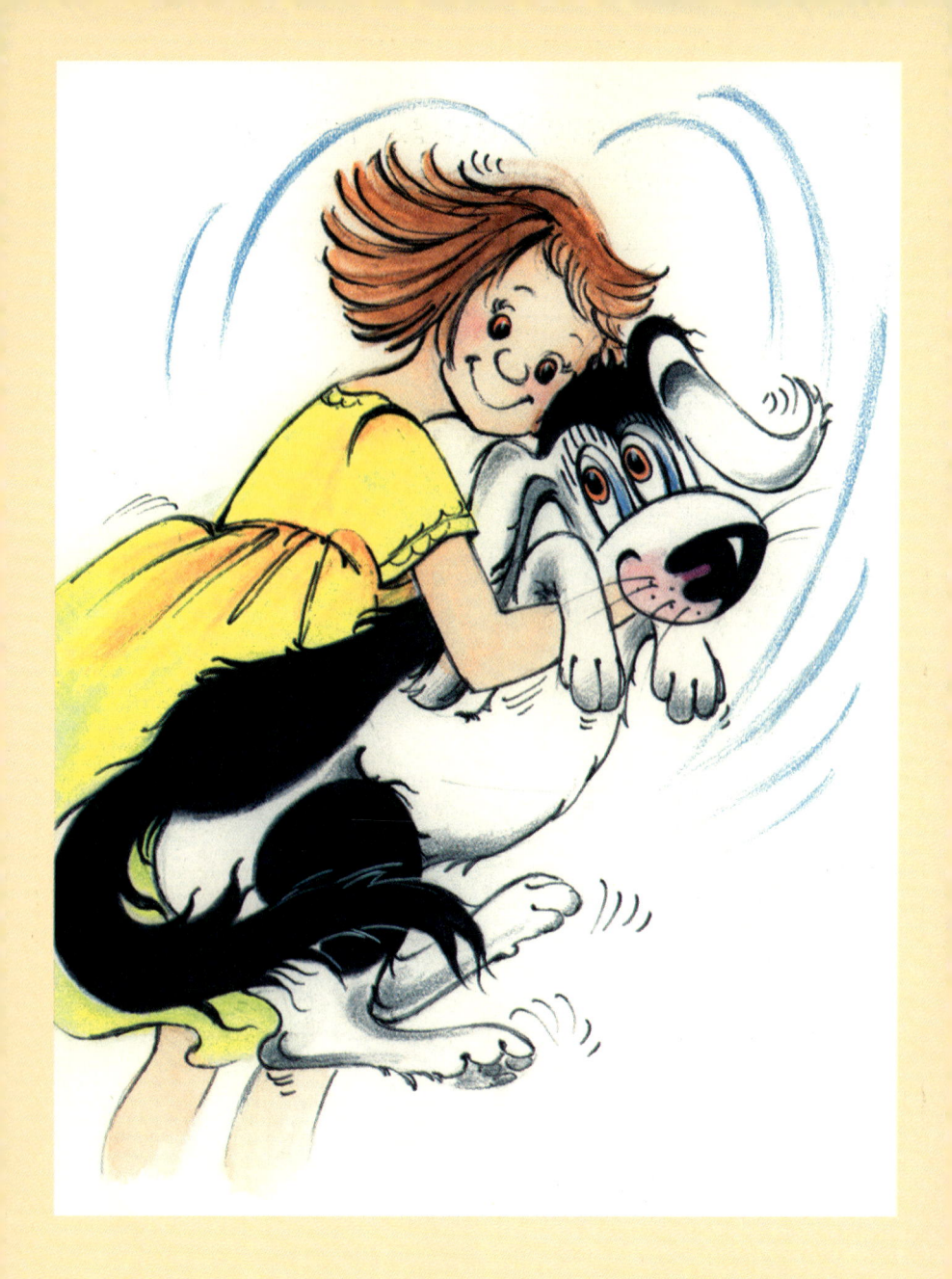

Patch is my best pet.